CW00801206

P

by Anne Jones

Foreword by H.E. Tsem Rinpoche

Published by Anne Jones
PO Box 7230, Burley, Ringwood, Hants, BH24 9EE,UK
Email: Anne@annejones.org
Website: www.annejones.org

Design: JackieHowchin.com
Printed by: Topcoatprint.com

ISBN: 978-0-9573627-1-0

About Anne Jones

Anne Jones has written a number of books published by Little Brown/Hatchetts on self development and how we can access our spiritual connections for happiness and inner strength. She lives in Burley, in the New Forest, UK with her husband Tony. She spends her time travelling around UK and overseas giving workshops, healing sessions and appears regularly on radio and TV. She is the founder of Hearts and Hands charity, Hearts and Hands Healing Organisation and Ripple Energy Therapy UK. For relaxation she walks the Forest with her Labradors, Harry and Supa.

www.annejones.org

Contents

4 Foreword by H.E. Tsem Rinpoche

7 Introduction

PART ONE – MANAGING NEGATIVITY
10 Chapter One - The Human Energy Field
18 Chapter Two - Ways to Protect Yourself
22 Chapter Three - Clearing Yourself and Space
28 Frequently Asked Questions

PART TWO – SETRAP THE PROTECTOR
30 Introduction
35 Who Needs Setrap?
36 About Setrap
44 Invoking Protection and Blessings

50 Index

FOREWORD

TSEM TULKU RINPOCHE
དགའ་ཤར་ཕུ་ལྦང་ཚེམས་སྤྲུལ་སྐུ།

Dearest Seekers,

In this day and age, with the advent of technology, activities in our lives and minds should have become easier and more convenient. Contrary to this, in fact, it has become more complicated, difficult and adverse.

In our daily lives, we have to deal with physical – as well as psychic – difficulties, problems and pollutants. Sometimes, we don't know where to turn to, where to go, or what to believe. Therefore, we try whatever we can, the best we can. There are many spiritual traditions and awakened Beings that we can contact in order to help us in our lives. But one with a lineage, a background and who is confirmed by thousands of years of practice and by many, many awakened masters will give us confidence. Protector Setrap is of that lineage.

Setrap comes from Gaden Shartse Monastery which was established 600 years ago in Tibet, in which He is still the chief Protector. Along with protecting Gaden Shartse, He has also been protecting many other monastic institutions, high Lamas, advanced yogis, great monks and teachers for the last 2,500 years, originating from a pure lineage in India.

Protector Setrap is known to be a fully awakened Being with complete omniscience and with consistent propitiation of this great Being, one will feel His protection, both psychic and physical, in our daily lives. Therefore, I am very happy to see a healer of world renown, with compassion in her heart, disseminating this great Protective Being.

I am elated and very, very happy to offer this foreword to Mrs Anne Jones who has been doing wonderful works and is now continuing her spiritual journey by sharing the sacred practice of Setrap to her friends of the past, present and future. Anne indeed cares deeply for the welfare and protection of her readers.

I offer my deepest felicitations and good wishes for the complete success of everyone's spiritual practice and of course, for Anne's work to grow even more in the future.

Tsem Rinpoche
Kechara
Kuala Lumpur

Introduction

If you wish to stand in your full power, if you want to work without feeling dominated by others, scared to speak out or drained by the neediness or dependency of those close to you then you need to consider protecting your energy on a daily basis.

If you help others through caring services, are a healer or therapist of any kind, work in a hospital, surgery or clinic, or are a member of the police, prison service or ambulance service you will need to protect yourself.

If you have a dominating parent, sibling or child, if any of the people at your place of work invade your space, bully you or disrespect you then you need to protect yourself.

If you work in the corporate world, large organisation or small company where there is competition, jealousy, self serving or prejudice then you will need to protect yourself.
You may be asking why? Why would you need to protect yourself and what form of

protection? Well, you need to protect yourself because your energy field is susceptible to the influence of other people's energy, emotions and thoughts. We are all connected by a common stream of energy so, therefore, we are affected by the moods of those near us. We are also affected by mass consciousness which is the accumulation of everybody's thoughts and emotions. This can lift us or, also, bring us down as you can experience when you go to a sporting event and your team is winning or losing. You can be affected by people living anywhere in the world and an event in any location.

In this book I will give you a number of ways that you can seal and strengthen your energy so you can be unaffected by these negative energies, whether they are inflicted on you unconsciously as is the case of people's moods and thoughts or consciously as in the case of black magic and curses.

Most importantly of all, I will share with you how to invoke and connect to Setrap, a most powerful spiritual protector, who was introduced to me by Tsem Rinpoche, a Tibetan Buddhist teacher, when I was being attacked by dark forces and in dire need of help. He has been my saviour.

Protection of your emotional, mental and spiritual energy is an antidote to the fear and anxiety that can affect you when you feel out of control of your circumstances or insecure. Of course, you will have to follow the practices diligently and also act with common sense. There is no protection in the world that will help you if you choose to step into the traffic with the mantra "the angels will protect me"!

So please take what I offer and use it and share it. Then you can get on with your life and work feeling safe and strong rather than insecure and weak. In other words take charge of the security of your energy and step into your full personal power and realise THE POWER OF YOU!

Love and blessings Anne

PART ONE – MANAGING NEGATIVITY
Chapter One

The Human Energy Field

The Aura, the energy field that flows through and around us, resonates and vibrates as a reflection of how we feel, our spiritual state, what we are thinking and our physical situation. It is a sensitive aspect of our total self and is easily affected by our own emotions, and those of other people. The closer emotionally and more toxic these people are the more they will affect us.

So, if you have a child who is going through a bad phase and taking drugs you can easily find yourself severely affected. In this situation you would be affected by your own fear, guilt, anger, shame etc. as well as your child's emotions of guilt, shame, fear and low esteem. You may become exhausted easily, feel depressed, feel anxious or be physically sick.

Thought-Forms

Every thought you have is a stream of your energy and resonates with your current emotional state. In the previous example - if you are angry with your child you will create a flow of low vibration (negative) energy that will attach to them as the focus of your thought. This will subsequently affect their energy field and bring their vibration down even further. On the other hand, if you are feeling loving and compassionate towards them then your thoughts will uplift them. We use this technique of sending love to people as a way of distant healing. It's powerful and effective. Anyone you think about will be affected by whatever you are feeling, either positive or negative.

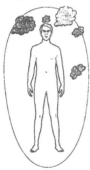

If you have a repetitive negative thought, e.g. worrying about a job, money or a family member, then this will accumulate and hang about you, rather like a dark cloud. Again, because of your holistic nature, this will affect you spiritually, emotionally, mentally and physically, e.g. stressful or worrying thoughts create a heavy thought-form that sits above you which in turn can give you a headache.

When an economic crisis or a disaster hits a community or country then the combined fearful and shocked feelings and thoughts of everyone affected will create an even bigger and more toxic thought-form. This in turn can affect those who are not even involved. So a disaster in one country can affect us all. When Diana, Princess of Wales was killed the thought-form of the British people affected many others around the world. On the upside the thrill and joy felt at the Olympic Games lifts all of us wherever we are.

Through our empathetic sense we feel for others and although this gives us a true sense of what others are feeling it can be a problem if we let it get out of control. Over a period of time we can experience side-effects of the problems of others and it can eventually affect our health.

How can you stop this?

Around your aura is an energy shield, a boundary, a border, that keeps your energy in place and prevents it from flowing here and there all over the place. Your boundary varies in effectiveness depending on your mood, your willpower and your sense of security. It also varies from person to person as some of us are more sensitive and open to other people's energies than others. If you have a job or a role that requires you to be aware of moods, atmospheres and feelings e.g. artist, nurse, carer, healer, poet etc. then you will be more open and sensitive to the energies around you. If you have to play a role where being open to emotion is a disadvantage then you will have developed a stronger and less sensitive boundary. E.g. People in armed forces, fire fighters, police etc. develop a thick skin to prevent them being immobilised by the emotions and events that they have to deal with.

Needy people can also drain your energy. Anyone who is depressed, insecure and feels that they are a victim will be inclined to draw energy from you. Their thoughts and feelings of dependency can create energy hooks that latch onto you. Through these energetic links they drain your energy. You may have noticed how tired you can be after spending time with someone who is going through difficulties. Counsellors and those who deal with people regularly in this situation need to be extra careful. It's one thing to offer support but you really do not want to have your energy drawn from you.

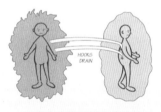

HOOKS FROM A NEEDY PERSON DRAIN YOUR ENERGY

I strongly advise everyone to reinforce their boundaries on a daily basis. By doing this you can preserve your own energy, prevent yourself from being manipulated or dominated and it will prevent you being disadvantaged by the effects of other people's issues. If you are in a situation where you are seriously affected by other people's negative intentions towards you then you will need a stronger protection and I will be addressing this situation in the chapter 2 on protection, but the minimum you need is a bubble. Use this every day and reinforce if, for example, you are going into a hospital which will be full of very needy people or visiting people who you know will challenge you!

The Bubble – *Re-enforcing your energy field boundary*
This is a simple but effective way to strengthen your natural energy boundary. Visualise a

bubble or egg shape and see yourself stepping into it. This sets your intention of strength-ening your natural energy boundary. This bubble will prevent the emotions and attitudes of other people from getting through to you.

If you cannot visualise say to yourself, "I am surrounded by a bubble that only allows light and positive energies to enter".

Saying No

If you are someone who finds it difficult to say "no", take note! If you have a caring and giving nature you may find it difficult to refuse other people's requests for time, attention and help. It is wonderful to help others and brings its rewards of love and fulfilment, but you have to make sure that you take care of yourself too. Avoid the compulsion to offer yourself and your time when you are very tired and ensure that you don't overstep from kindness into self-sacrifice. Learn to say "no" when your own needs are compromised otherwise you will burn out. Then you will be unable to help anyone!

Anyone in the caring profession is likely to forget this from time to time – just watch out for the signs which are unreasonable fatigue and a sense of being drained by the people you are helping.

Remember to respect yourself, care for yourself and create your own boundaries and hold firm to them.

Chapter Two
Protecting yourself

You will be pleased to know that there are a number of ways to keep your energy field and yourself safe. I will share some of my favourites here and you can decide which ones suit you best. You can also use them for your family and friends but as with all spiritual practises it is most beneficial if the one that needs the protection follows the practise personally. I have successfully used all the methods I am sharing here so can recommend all of them. Every day I say prayers to Setrap (see Part Two), but I also use the bubble as a shield against other people's emotions when I feel the need and I use the Blue Flame before a healing session and before I sleep.

The Blue Flame of Archangel Michael- *protect against negative spiritual activity; peaceful sleep*
This energy flame that has been gifted to us by the Protector Archangel Michael (you will see him often depicted carrying a sword in religious paintings). The flame creates a shield

that allows only positive energies such as love to come through to you. Visualise yourself surrounded by a blue flame and do this first thing in the morning. As spirit activity can interfere with us at night I recommend you re-seal with the flame before you go to sleep to ensure a clear and untroubled night.

Protection Symbol – *keeping yourself and your possessions safe*

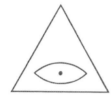

This symbol creates a shield around a person or object. My clients have very effectively used the amulet I have created from this to protect their animals, family and possessions. Draw on paper or in the air from the base up with two hands and finish with the "eye" in the centre. It creates a pyramid which in itself is a powerful protection.

Four Trees – *powerful against psychic attack*
I used this when I was once chased through the streets of Hong Kong by a demonic energy that

had attached to one of my clients! Visualise four large trees set around you. Then see gold chains wrapped around the trees; finally see a white light shining down onto you.

Essential Oils – *Create an atmosphere of strength and protection for you and your home*
Essential plant oils Juniper-berry, Rosemary, Laurel, Pine and Cedar wood will uplift and strengthen your energy field. I have created a spray called Protection from these oils that I use when I am giving healing sessions (find them on www.annejones.org).

Crystals – *To strengthen your aura and create a protective field. Use as jewellery, in your home and on computers and electronic equipment.*
Obsidian, black tourmaline, jasper and malachite are just a few of the crystals that will create a protective field and strengthen your own aura when you wear them. You need to cleanse your crystals regularly as they will absorb negativity. E.g. wash in sea salt and energise either in the sun or on a large amethyst.

White Light – *using divine love and angels*
This is a popular method of protection used by therapists and healers as it's quick and simple. Ask for help from your angels – Archangel Michael is devoted to our protection – and call in divine white light to surround you.

The Violet Flame – *transform negativity*
The Violet Flame was given to us by the Ascended Master Saint Germaine. It will transform any negativity you may have picked up or created and will also protect you. Either visualise it burning around you or say "I am surrounded by the Violet Flame". Your intention will create it around you.

Attitude – *appear strong, hide your weakness*
Bullies in physical or spiritual form will always look for weakness. What is your Achilles heal, where can you be caught off guard? Work on your issue or problem and then you will be less vulnerable. Create the impression that you are strong even when you feel weak. Finally laugh; find the humour in even the worst situation - it lifts and disperses negativity brilliantly!

Chapter Three
Clearing Yourself and Space

If you haven't used effective protection there may be times when your aura can become "infected" by negative energies. These can come from many sources; other people's thoughts, hooks from the needy and dependant or spirit energy that latches onto you for its own needs (the spirit of an addict will search out living addicts to fulfil its craving as these can still linger after death if a spirit does not go to the heavenly realms). Other sources are the energies that are released when healing, the fears and anxieties of the public or curses and worse put onto you by users of black magic. It is, therefore, useful to know of ways to clear your personal energy field and to cleanse yourself of long term or short term infiltration and attachments.

Your home and workplace can also be affected. If you or your family have been going through difficult times the energy of your home can hold these low and heavy vibrations. Furniture, paintings and the walls themselves can retain negative energy. In a workplace where there have been difficulties, visits from the public or at the site of a traumatic event there is likely to be negative contamination. Here are a number of ways that you can resolve these problems for yourself and your living and working space.

Smudging

You can use the smoke from herbs to clear yourself or space. White Sage is a herb that contains powerful cleansing properties and is perfect for this use. You can buy specially prepared bundles of dried sage specifically for this purpose. Light the end of the bundle but knock out any flames; when it is just smouldering take it around the building and waft the smoke into every corner. You can blow on the embers to increase the volume of smoke and use a large bird feather to direct the smoke – this is the traditional method used by North American Indians who have used smudging as a way to purify and heal for centuries. You can also use smudging to clear yourself, clothes, furniture and jewellery.

Frankincense which is a resin also has very powerful cleansing properties. The smoke reacts with negative energies and transforms them. I knew a space clearer who would visit the accounts department of a company he was helping and burn Frankincense to detect any negative energies emanating from the files of suppliers. The colour of the smoke became darker when negativity was detected. In the case of suppliers it indicated that they were cheating the company in some way!

Essential Oils

Plant oils have many healing properties. For clearing energies you can use good quality, preferably organic, oils in a burner, with reed diffusers or as a spray. The most effective oils for clearing space are peppermint, sage, juniper berry, and cedar wood. I have a spray created by Ripple UK "Clear and Cleanse." (See end of book for more details). Before I had my own sprays, I used juniper oil and showered with a lime bath gel to clear my aura. I cleared my healing room by smudging with sage and burning sandalwood incense.

Incense
Traditionally in churches and temples incense has been used to purify the atmosphere and ward of negative entities. Sandalwood is my favourite and is easily available.

Salt
Sea salt is an excellent absorber of negative energy and I have cleared rooms simply by sprinkling the salt around the perimeter then smudging. I also put a bowl of water containing sea salt in my healing room to clear the energies released in the healing sessions.

Symbol to clear thought-forms of fear
 This symbol can be used to clear thought-forms created by fear or anxiety. You can clear a room by visualising this spinning, enveloping and transforming negative clouds. Draw from the top left hand and finish with the circle.

Visualisation

Here is an easy meditation you can use to clear away negative thought-forms, blocks and attachments:

- Close your eyes and ground yourself by seeing yourself as a great tree with roots growing into the ground and fully connecting with Planet Earth.
- See a white vortex of swirling energy like a mini tornado coming down into the top of your head and enveloping you.
- As it spins it proceeds down your body and clears your energy as it spins.
- It gradually clears all thought-forms, all attachments and takes them down into the centre of the Earth to be transformed into light.

I have a recorded version on my CD Healing Visualisations and it is also available on YouTube – AnneJonesHealer, Clearing Negative Thought-forms.

Sweeping away hooks

Needy and dependant people can attach hooks into your aura and drain your energy. You can either clear these yourself by rubbing an essential oil such as juniper on your hands then sweeping your shoulders and back with the intention of clearing them. Or ask a friend or colleague to do this for you. They should first protect their energy by sealing with the Blue Flame.

Burning – let the flames transform the energy
Many of your own negative emotions will come from past wrongs or longing for people who are no longer in your life. To prevent the thought-forms of grief, yearning, anger, bitterness and guilt to build you need to release the emotions that surround these thoughts. Write down all you think and feel about the situation or person. Give full vent and write everything, no matter how negative. Then have a ceremonial burning and know that all the attachments and all the thought-forms are leaving you and turning into light as the flames burn the paper and transform and release your supressed emotions.

F.A.Q

Q. How do I know if the feelings I am experiencing are from my own fears and self-created thought-forms and demons or if I am under psychic attack or black magic?

A. If you are affected by negativity from outside of you, whether it's from someone's jealous thoughts or full blown black magic, you will not feel it when you are standing under a shower or waterfall. The flowing water will shield you so you can test out your situation quite easily this way.

Q. In my meditation I get spirits talking to me and offering to help me. Should I listen?

A. Ask them if they stand in divine light, or The Christ Light. If they answer anything other than a direct yes then do not continue to listen to them. Ask this question four times. By spiritual law they have to answer honestly.

Q. I think I am cursed. What can I do about this?

A. You can ask for help from someone who specialises in clearing such negativity. (e.g. The

Taost Temple in Malaysia see end of the book).
I suggest you use the prayers and mantras of
the Protector Setrap (Part Two). Practise them
daily and he will protect you from any negative
forces that may be affecting you.

Q. I think my house if affected by negative
energies, how can I check this out?
A. A space clearing practitioner can dowse at a
distance to check the energy status of a
building. In my book Healing Negative Energies
I give instructions how you can do this for
yourself. I suggest you use the techniques in
the next chapter and if you still feel the energy
is depleted or disturbed get professional help.
e.g. Debbie Rye in UK (details at end of book).

Q. Can I send any bad vibes that I receive back
to the sender?
A. The best place to send these energies is to
the light. Then they can be transformed and
will not harm anyone else in the future. Use
your intention to do this. Say "I send all
energies that are not positive to the light, now,
right now."

PART TWO – SETRAP THE PROTECTOR
Introduction

Before I introduce the Protector Setrap let me share my own experience of how I came to be introduced to him and his amazing powers.

Some time ago I realised that I was the subject of a severe and serious psychic attack. I had suspected for some time that there were dark forces trying to shut me down and hold me back from doing my work. I had felt physically attacked on one occasion in Japan which resulted in a fall with my luggage on an escalator at Narita Airport. I was saved by the quick action of other travellers who shut down the escalator and helped me and my luggage up to the top. I just knew that I hadn't fallen, my feet had been firmly on the step; I sensed I had been pushed and later this was to be confirmed for me.

I recovered from the fall but a short time later as I was about to leave for my annual visit to Malaysia to give workshops and sessions I received a call from the organiser, Jennifer

Khoo. She was upset and told me there were no bookings for my main workshop, there were hardly any sessions booked and my other workshops had only one booking! Shock! This surprised us both as my numbers are normally nearer 80 than zero! I knew then that something dark was working against me. Jen offered to consult a man called Jo who specialises in clearing negative spirits and black magic. He is based at the Taoist temple in Penang, in the north of Malaysia. Jo and his fellow devotees at the temple work with a group of Taoist celestial masters; deities who work in spirit to clear the most negative of forces from people and space. They discovered that I was being stalked by a demonic entity that planned to harm me physically and close down my work. As this resonated with both myself and Jen I decided to ask for help.

Jen set up a couple of very important meetings for me. The first was with Jo from the Penang temple. He cleared my energy and re-connected me to my own spiritual master – Kwan Yin, who has been working with me for over twenty years. The second was with Tsem Rinpoche, the spiritual leader of The Kechara Buddhist Organisation in Kuala Lumpur. He introduced me to Setrap Chen his own dharma protector* and the one used by the monks of his monastery, Gaden Shartse, established in Tibet 600 years ago. He taught me the sacred texts that monks and Lamas have used for over 2,500 years to protect themselves and their work in India, in Tibet and subsequently in their monasteries and centres where they now work around the world. He also encouraged me to share the powerful words through my own work, as you will have read in his foreword for this book.

Since that time I have not been bothered by my stalking demon nor has my work been compromised. I say the prayer and repeat the mantra daily and I give thanks through the tea offering. I use the dedication of these prayers for protection for myself, my family, for my work and my students. I request abundance to allow me to continue my work; I ask for assistance for healing those who have approached me for help. Setrap Chen is a supreme being and uses his powers not only to act as a guardian giving us protection but also clears away any obstacles in our way – what could be better than that!

I encourage you to also make use of this powerful spiritual protector and to share with anyone you know who may need his services. He is all powerful but you need to make the connection yourself through your prayers and mantras, then he will respond to your requests.

Purifying

In the days after I first started to make the connection to Setrap and asked for his help I had a series of dreams, almost nightmares, of buildings collapsing, floods, chaos and destruction. Rinpoche told me this was a clearing and cleansing process is quite normal. You may find that this happens to you – if not as dreams but as physical detoxifying. Know that is a purifying process and that once the negativity has gone you will feel better and your life will be more peaceful.

Dedication

Just remember to always dedicate your mantras and prayers once you have finished saying them otherwise they may get stolen by any passing spirit for its own purpose – such a waste! If you have any questions on Setrap I suggest you direct these to Kechara and the true experts on this wonderful deity. www.kechara.com

Finally, don't be alarmed at the imagery of Setrap, his fierce looks are to frighten away your detractors. His actual energy is very beautiful, loving and supportive.

A Dharma Protector (Dharmapala) is an emanation of a Buddha who clears the inner and outer obstacles that prevent practitioners from gaining spiritual progress, also supporting them for the fulfillment of their objectives and work.

Who Needs Help From Setrap?

I recommend everyone to connect to Setrap but he is particularly helpful if you are in any of these situations:

- Struggling with blocks on your spiritual path
- Finding it difficult to pursue your chosen dream or goal
- Attacked by black magic or voodoo
- You sense you are under a curse or spell
- Affected by the negative energies of others
- Working in dangerous situations or locations
- Under attack from the media or gossip
- Apprehensive of new projects or ventures
- Living with negative family members
- Threatened mentally, emotionally or physically
- Bothered by voices or negative thoughts
- Suffering nightmares or troubled sleep
- Living in a location where satanic or occult ceremonies are practised

- You have a mission to care for people, animals or the planet
- You work in the judiciary system
- You are an activist for human rights
- If you work in a mental institution or prison
- You have been abused or attacked
- You sense hidden dangers around you
- You are a spiritual leader or teacher
- Concerned about the safety of your family
- Your business or work is in difficulty
- Your feel weak or insecure
- You are a celebrity or hold a prominent position
- You work as a carer or therapist
- You are holding the light and shining it into the world in your own unique way!

I suggest you start by using the mantra and as you feel comfortable with this start the prayer and offering. I repeat it when I am driving, walking, waiting for someone – it is a great way to make sure your time is never wasted! The traditional way to repeat mantras is to us Mala beads. These are like a rosary and have two purposes. They come in strings of 108 beads and you can use them to count the number of mantras you say. Secondly the energy of the mantra flows into the beads as you speak and so you create a protective talisman that you can carry around with you. You can create your own set of beads or if you wish to purchase one that has been blessed go to a Buddhist shop or website. The Kechara Centre, which is Rinpoche's organisation in Malaysia has a range made from crystal and gemstones (see at the end of the book).

 The more you use the mantra and the prayers the stronger your connection to Setrap will become. The words themselves hold powerful vibrations so say them out loud. The mantra, which is in Tibetan, has been used over 2,500 years and is empowered by all the monks and high Lamas who have recited it millions of times.

SETRAP

A brief description of Setrap:

- The red colour of Setrap's body symbolises control over one's inner and outer environments.
- The overbite of the lower-lip symbolises control of one's faculties.
- Setrap has three luminous, penetrating eyes that represent seeing into the phenomena of the past, present and future, unobstructed.
- His right hand raises a divine cudgel representing the elimination of our obstacles, pains, guilt and troubles.
- The left hand holds a lasso bound to a 'human'; the binding of this 'human' represents the binding of all of our fears, destructive attitudes, self-created delusions and demons.
- He wears the armaments of a 'leather cuirass' likened to when we go into battle and wear armaments to protect ourselves; this represents that Setrap has incredible protective abilities for us.

- The psychic flames which arise from every pore of His body symbolise that wherever He abides, there is an impenetrable force of protection.
- The horse He rides is not a physical animal but an avatar of His mind, representing swiftness in fulfilling our spiritual quests.
- The diadem of 'skulls' is a reminder of the fallacious notion of permanency and the ever-present specter of our own demise; hence, it reminds us to put full energy into our spiritual growth. This diadem of 'skulls' also symbolises that He will benefit the dearly departed when we pray for them.
- The five victory flags mounted on His helmet represents generosity, contentment, wisdom, stability and growth.

How Setrap's practice can help you

- Setrap will help us on an immediately worldly level to answer our prayers. He will remove obstacles in our daily lives and provide good conditions for whatever we need – e.g. health, finances, family, harmony, jobs, business and wealth
- On a higher level, Setrap clears the way for us to be able to do spiritual practice with no obstruction and to gain wisdom to be able to help ourselves and overcome our own problems in the long term.
- Our motivation is very important when we pray to Setrap. If we are praying for things that will harm ourselves or others, Setrap will not answer those prayers.
- Setrap's practice is very effective for protection and clearing negative interferences in your homes – e.g. spirit disturbances or "bad energy".
- Setrap is a fully enlightened Buddha (he is Amitabha), so when you make offerings and prayers to him, you can purify a lot of negative karma and gain a lot of merit

needed to support your spiritual work, practice and aspirations.

- You can also do Setrap's practice to be dedicated to your loved ones, family and anyone who needs help.
- Setrap's prayers can also help you to gain a lot of peace and clarity in your own mind and heart.
- It is important to think that when you are doing the prayers, that Setrap is really there and that he hears our prayers. Having faith and trust is an important factor.
- Also, have faith that whatever the outcome of our prayers, Setrap bestows on us what will be most beneficial, *not* what we think we need or what we want. For example, we may pray for a relationship. But if a relationship will not serve us on the highest level and will be detrimental to us in the long term, Setrap may not give it to us.
- Sometimes, when we start engaging in Protector practices, it might seem like things go wrong for awhile. E.g. we might

get sick, have arguments, accidents, or even a loss of finances. Do not be alarmed. This is necessary sometimes as a kind of spiritual "detox". For example, when we engage in a detox program for our bodies, we might sometimes have diarrhoea, nausea, headaches etc. – this is expected as it is a purging out of toxins and things that are harmful to our body. It is similar for spiritual practices. It is sometimes necessary to clear out the bad before the good can arise.

Setrap Prayer and Mantra.

To show your commitment to your request for help from Setrap it is traditional practise to offer black tea. You can prepare this and place it in front of you before you start your prayers. Also, following traditional practise, I light sweet smelling incense and a candle and put these before my picture of Setrap.

Once you have completed your prayers put out your dedications – your requests for help.

Invoking Protection and Blessings

A Prayer to Setrap.

Composed by H.E. Tsem Rinpoche

Among many worlds, realms and dimensions
Abide countless awakened beings, enlightened masters
And those we call upon as having full omniscience.

From among these beings, we request Setrap,
The Cosmic Warrior who rides on a gallant horse,
Traversing the winds of karma and
Galloping across various dimensions *sans* creation,
To come to this place at this time.

Setrap, Your appearance is that of a powerful, strong, divine General
Although Your heart abides in complete compassion.
Your fierce appearance is only to grant protection and
Dispel those who would be harmers.
Please abide here with me now.

I offer You a libation of incense and flowers,
And pure water and teas and all that is wonderful,
Free of attachments, that exists in the universe,
actual and visualised.
Please partake of the libation of tea
And the various other sensory offerings I have
placed
In order for me to make a strong affinity with You.
(say this verse 3 times)

Regrets, mistakes and deeds done of ignorance
Which may haunt my mind bringing self-doubt and
remorse,
I ask You to cleanse as I have learnt and progressed.
May they not bear unwanted sorrows.

My body, environment, mind
Are subject to fears, self-ridicule, pain,
degeneration,
Illness, old age, spiritual and psychic pollutions.
It all arises from grasping at an illusionary ego
Which clouds our perceptions.

Great Cosmic Warrior Setrap!
Send forth unlimited rays of purifying light, entering
my body,
Clearing me of disease and fears,

And granting me light, love, freedom and
compassion.

Cosmic Being, who travels existence in a single
instant,
I request You to abide in this place, in this house,
In this abode, in this land, in this area and in my
heart.
May no negative forces or legions of harm and
damage enter.

Please grant Your sacred diamond-like* protection,
That is immovable, indestructible and unassailable,
To my environment and to the beings therein
I request of You.

Grant us protection, blessings,
Together with signs and auspicious dreams
Of Your holy presence in this abode.

May our works, our lives, our bounty increase,
So that we may be of service to others.
May everyone who abides in this abode
Have bountiful growth, prosperity
And spiritual, along with worldly wealth, if it suits
them.

Whenever I travel, am at home, working or in
various activities,
Please grant thorough protection,
Like a body followed by its shadow,
To never be separated from You and Your cosmic
emanations.
**May You, and all holy and divine and powerful
That abide in Your sacred, ruby-like mandala also
bless us.

May my channels, my pathways, chakras
And every single ligament, bone, artery, muscle and
fibre
In my body be blessed.
May all my chakras open,
Be healed, be filled with light and be unobstructed
So that I may gain the divine, compassion, wisdom,
Skilful means and full omniscience, just like Yourself.

I dedicate my prayers and my solicitations to You
That the world may be at peace,
All countries may have harmony.
May all the animals be safe, the waters be clear,
The environment become pure.
May all leaders decide for the benefit of others,
May all citizens have more concern for their
neighbours than themselves,

May all that exists always abide in light, life and
happiness
And our planet and all planets be safe.

I now chant Your sacred mantra,
Which are the sounds of power, compassion, skillful
means,
Healing, meditation and wisdom.

And as I chant and recite Your holy mantra
May the reverberations and vibrations of the
mantra
Pervade my body, my mind, my soul,
And everyone that I love,
May it even pervade those I view as enemies,
Be filled with love, light, forgiveness, protection
Growth, awareness and Enlightenment.

Setrap, I keep You close to my heart
Grant me full protection from all that may be
harmful
To me, my work, loved ones, environment
And especially my Enlightenment.

Setrap's mantra:

OM MA-HA YAK-CHA TSA SO-HA
*(Recite daily 7 times, 21 times or more,
depending on your time and schedule. Of
course, the more the better.)*

*Colophon: At the request of Ms. Anne Jones, this
prayer was composed by H.E. Tsem Rinpoche on 18
August 2012, in Kuala Lumpur, Malaysia, for the
protection and blessings of all spiritual practitioners.*

© Tsem Rinpoche
Notes:
*In this case, diamonds represent indestructibility.
**Within Setrap's sacred space abide a multitude of
holy, awakened Beings and assistants, angels,
dakinis and dakas. We are requesting all their
blessings.

After your prayers don't forget
to make your requests.

Index

abundance, 35
accidents, 48
addict, 23
ambulance service, 7
amethyst, 21
Amitabha, 46
anxiety, 9, 27
Archangel Michael, 19, 22
arguments, 48
armed forces, 14
artist, 14
attachments, 23, 28, 29
Attitude, 22
aura, 14, 21, 23, 28
Aura, 11
black magic, 8, 23, 30, 39
black tourmaline, 21
blocks, 28, 39
Blue Flame, 19, 29
boundary, 14, 16
bubble, 16, 19
Bubble, 16
Buddha, 38, 46
Bullies, 22

bully, 7
Burning, 29
business, 40, 46
carer, 14, 40
cedar wood, 25
Cedar wood, 21
Christ Light, 30
Clear and Cleanse, 25
clearing, 25, 29, 30, 46, 58
Clearing Negative Thought-forms, 28
Clearing Yourself and Space, 23
clinic, 7
corporate, 7
Counsellors, 15
Crystals, 21
curse, 39
cursed, 30
curses, 8, 23
dedication, 35
demonic energy, 20
demons, 30
Dharma, 38

Dharma Protector, 38

Dharmapala, 38, 64

distant healing, 12

dominating parent, 7

dowse, 31

egg, 16

energy field, 8, 11, 12, 19, 21, 23

Energy Field, 3, 11

Essential Oils, 21, 25

F.A.Q, 30

fear, 9, 11, 27

fears, 23, 30

finances, 46, 48

Four Trees, 20

Frankincense, 25

Gaden, 35

headache, 13

headaches, 48

healer, 7, 14

health, 14, 46

hooks, 23, 28

hospital, 7, 16

Incense, 27

jasper, 21

jealousy, 7

juniper berry,, 25

Juniper-berry, 21

karma, 46

Kechara, 35, 38

Kwan Yin, 35

Laurel, 21

malachite, 21

mantra, 9, 35, 40

mass consciousness, 8

needy, 16, 23

new projects, 39

nightmares, 39

nurse, 14

Obsidian, 21

obstacles, 36, 38, 46

occult, 39

peppermint, 25

Pine, 21

poet, 14

police, 7, 14

prison, 7, 40

prison service, 7

Protecting yourself, 19

protection, 8, 16, 19, 20, 21, 22, 23, 36, 46

Protection, 9, 16, 20, 62

psychic attack, 20, 30, 33

pyramid, 20

relationship, 47

Rosemary, 21

sage, 24, 25

Salt, 27

Sandalwood, 27

satanic, 39

sea salt, 21, 27

sensitive, 11, 14

Setrap, 3, 19, 31, 33, 35, 36, 38, 39, 41, 46, 47, 64

SETRAP, 3, 33, 43

Smudging, 24

spell, 39

spiritual leader, 35, 40

spiritual path, 39

spiritual practice, 46

surgery, 7

Taoist temple, 34

Taost Temple, 31

therapist, 7, 40

thought-forms, 27, 28, 29, 30

Thought-Forms, 12

Tsem Rinpoche, 1, 3, 9, 35

Violet Flame, 22

wealth, 46

White Light, 22

White Sage, 24

References

Debbie Rye – distant diagnosis and clearing of negative energies. www.alternativeways.co.uk dar@alternativeways.co.uk.

Hearts and Hands Healing Organisation
For distance healing and counselling support.
www.annejones.org.

Toaist Temple, Penang, Malaysia. Contact Jo by text
+60 124382790

Anne Jones on YouTube
Visit annejoneshealer YouTube for Anne's videos of meditations and healing negative energy sessions.

E-Course – Clear and Protect Your Energy
If you are interested in learning more about transforming and protecting yourself from negative energies Anne has produced an E-course The Power of You – Clear and Protect Your Energy. You will find details on her website: www.annejones.org

For information on Tsem Rinpoche and his work:
Personal blog: blog.tsemtulku.com
Official website: tsemtulku.com
Facebook: facebook.com/TsemTulkuRinpoche
YouTube: youtube.com/tsemtulku
Twitter: twitter.com/tsemtulku

For information on Kechara, Tsem Rinpoche's organisation in Malaysia:
Official website: kechara.com
Facebook: facebook.com/kecharahouse
Email: care@kechara.com

For information on Setrap
Setrap the Protector, by Tsem Rinpoche and Sharon Saw
A box set containing a book about Setrap's history and his practice, two prayer books and a beautiful, portable image of Setrap.

The box set, pendants, images, prints and other blessed items of Setrap can be obtained on the online store **vajrasecrets.com**

Further teachings on Setrap on YouTube: visit youtube.com/tsemtulku and search "Setrap"

ANNE JONES
Healing
Negative
Energies

SIMPLE STEPS TO
IMPROVE YOUR ENERGY
AT HOME AND AT WORK

*You will find further information about managing
and controlling the effects of negative energies in
Anne Jones's book, Healing Negative Energies,
published by Piatkus of Little Brown Books, available
from Amazon.co.uk, bookstores and
www.annejones.org.*

ANNE JONES
The Power of You

SIMPLE STEPS TO OVERCOME FEAR
AND REGAIN STRENGTH
AND CONFIDENCE

You will find further help for developing your personal power in Anne Jones's book, The Power of You, published by Piatkus of Little Brown Books, available from Amazon.co.uk, bookstores and www.annejones.org.

Anne Jones books

Published by Piatkus of Little Brown Books
Heal Yourself
Healing Negative Energies
The Ripple Effect
Opening Your Heart
The Soul Connection
The Power of You
A6 pocket book – Heal and be Healed
There are CDs of the guided meditations in the books

Essential Oil Sprays by Anne Jones

Clearing and Cleansing
Protection
Spiritual Connection
Opening your Heart

For Your Protection

The Protection symbol silver with obsidian.
Available as a pendant, earrings or key-chain

**All products are available from
www.annejones.org**